FIVE TIPS TO SIMPLIFY ENTRIES

The Importance of the Link Card

Audrey Grant

Five Tips to Simplify Entries
The Importance of the Link Card

Baron Barclay
3600 Chamberlain Lane, Suite 206
Louisville, KY 40241
U.S. and Canada: 1-800-274-2221
Worldwide: 502-426-0140
Fax: 502-426-2044
www.baronbarclay.com

Contact the author at:
betterbridge@betterbridge.com

ISBN 978-1-944201-28-9

Design and composition by David Lindop

Contents

Introduction

Entries are frequently overlooked, yet they're important for effective declarer play. Five Tips to Simplify Entries is divided into two parts and includes useful features for accessing the information.

Part I – An Introduction to the Five Tips

In each segment in Part I, a tip to simplify entries is introduced. Extra deals are included in Part I to illustrate the tips.

Part II - A Collection of Instructional Deals

The basic and finer points of entries are introduced through sixteen carefully constructed deals. The first five in the collection are straightforward and each one represents another example of the five tips. The deals become more challenging as you progress. Deals #15 and #16, the Famous Deals, show how world-class players handle entries.

The Bridge Quiz

On the odd-numbered pages, the Instructional Deals are shown in a Bridge Quiz format. The Suggested Bidding, Opening Lead and the first steps in Planning the Play are given. The Bridge Quiz poses a challenge for the declarer to decide how to play the deal. Turn the page to see the Suggested Play and the Conclusion.

Bookmarks

For easy reference, essential ideas are summarized on the four Bookmarks attached to the front and back covers.

The Declarer's Plan Bookmark, attached to the front cover, can help declarer make a habit of using the plan before playing to the first trick. This Bookmark can be placed over the even-numbered pages, starting on page 14, opposite the Bridge Quiz on page 15.

The Five Tips to Simplify Entries Bookmark is attached to the back cover. It can be placed over the odd-numbered pages when reading the answer to a Bridge Quiz as a reminder of the specific tip being applied.

There are two reference Bookmarks: one is the Probability of Suit Distributions in the Defenders' Hands, and the other, a summary on Blocking and Unblocking.

The Glossary

Italicized words in the text are defined in the Glossary, with page references for where the terms first appear.

The Publishing

The Audrey Grant Bridge Guide series is published with the reader in mind. The two-color printing highlights the hearts and diamonds in red, making the book easier to read. The binding method allows the front and back covers to be put together without harming the book. This makes it possible for the book to lay flat on the table.

We hope you enjoy your adventure with entries. Thank you for being part of Better Bridge.

Audrey Grant and the Better Bridge Team

PART I

AN INTRODUCTION TO THE FIVE TIPS

Low Cards as Entries

To get the most out of the trick-taking potential of a deal, understanding entries is necessary. They are important whether you have enough tricks to make the contract, or need to develop extra tricks. Let's start with a practical word to describe an *entry*.

L'ENTRY

An entry is usually considered a high card that gives declarer a way to get from declarer's hand to the dummy or vice versa. An entry has two parts. There is the *winner* in the hand you are trying to reach, and the lower-ranking *link card* that provides transportation to the entry. The "L" in *L'Entry* is a reminder that the lower-ranking link card is as important as the higher-ranking entry.

Consider the following *suit combinations*:

1)	DUMMY	2)	DUMMY
	♦ A K Q J		♦ A K Q J
	DECLARER		DECLARER
	♦ 3		♦ –

In the first layout, dummy's high cards provide four tricks. The ♦3 in declarer's hand provides a link to the diamonds in the dummy. In the second layout, there is no link card in declarer's hand to get to the four potential diamond winners in dummy. The winners are *stranded* unless there is an entry to dummy in another suit.

It's essential to realize that an entry is a relationship between two cards. One is the higher-ranking entry card, and the other is the lower-ranking link card.

Most of the time, high cards such as aces, kings and queens are used as entries. Much lower cards can also serve as entries if declarer has a lower-ranking card that can be used as a link card.

Consider the following deal. South is the declarer in 3NT and West leads the ♠K:

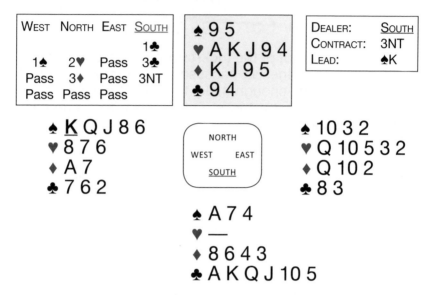

WEST	NORTH	EAST	SOUTH
			1♣
1♠	2♥	Pass	3♣
Pass	3♦	Pass	3NT
Pass	Pass	Pass	

♠ 9 5
♥ A K J 9 4
♦ K J 9 5
♣ 9 4

DEALER:	SOUTH
CONTRACT:	3NT
LEAD:	♠K

♠ K Q J 8 6
♥ 8 7 6
♦ A 7
♣ 7 6 2

NORTH
WEST   EAST
SOUTH

♠ 10 3 2
♥ Q 10 5 3 2
♦ Q 10 2
♣ 8 3

♠ A 7 4
♥ —
♦ 8 6 4 3
♣ A K Q J 10 5

Declarer needs nine tricks and has a spade, two hearts, and six clubs. Unfortunately, there is no link card to the heart winners in the dummy, so declarer needs to find an entry in another suit.

There is another problem. Once the ♠A is driven out, declarer can't afford to let the opponents gain the lead before declarer takes nine tricks.

After winning the ♠A, declarer plays the lower-ranking link card, the ♣5 to dummy's ♣9 and then takes the two heart winners, the ♥A and ♥K. The ♣4 is the link card to get back to the remaining club winners in declarer's hand. Declarer takes nine tricks.

The first tip to simplify entries is:

Tip #1:   Recognize a low card as an entry by keeping a lower-ranking link card.

High Cards as Link Cards

Just as a low card can be an entry provided there is a lower-ranking link card in the opposite hand, a high card can act as a link card provided there is a higher-ranking entry in the opposite hand.

Consider the following heart layouts:

1)   DUMMY
        ♥ K Q J 10

        DECLARER
        ♥ A

2)   DUMMY
        ♥ A Q J 10

        DECLARER
        ♥ K

In the first layout, even though declarer has all the top hearts, the suit will provide only one trick unless there is an entry to dummy in another suit. The suit is *blocked* since there is no link card in the heart suit after the ♥A is played. The remaining three heart winners in the dummy are stranded.

In the second layout, declarer again has all the top hearts but can take four heart tricks without needing an entry in another suit. Declarer can use the ♥K as a link card to dummy by *overtaking* it with dummy's ♥A.

Sometimes suits can be *partially blocked*. Consider the following example:

DUMMY
♥ A Q J 2

DECLARER
♥ K

To get four heart tricks from this layout, declarer needs an entry in another suit. If declarer needs only three heart tricks and has no outside entry to dummy, declarer can use the ♥K as the link card to get to dummy's ♥A. Then declarer takes the winning ♥Q-J.

Consider the following deal. South is the declarer in 4♥ and West leads the ♦K:

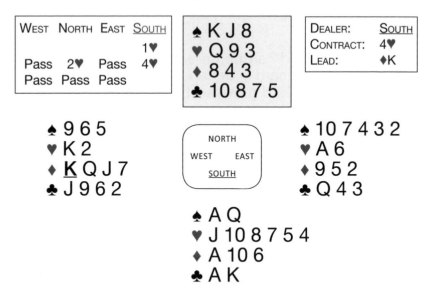

West	North	East	South
			1♥
Pass	2♥	Pass	4♥
Pass	Pass	Pass	

♠ K J 8
♥ Q 9 3
♦ 8 4 3
♣ 10 8 7 5

Dealer: South
Contract: 4♥
Lead: ♦K

♠ 9 6 5
♥ K 2
♦ K Q J 7
♣ J 9 6 2

NORTH
WEST   EAST
SOUTH

♠ 10 7 4 3 2
♥ A 6
♦ 9 5 2
♣ Q 4 3

♠ A Q
♥ J 10 8 7 5 4
♦ A 10 6
♣ A K

Declarer has two heart *losers*, the ♥A-K, and two diamond losers, the ♦Q-J. That's one too many.

After the ♦A is driven out, declarer has four quick losers and can't afford to give up the lead. If declarer draws trumps, the defenders will win the ♥A and ♥K and immediately take their two established diamond winners.

Fortunately, declarer has an extra spade winner in dummy on which a diamond loser can be discarded.

After winning the ♦A, declarer can take a trick with the ♠A and then use the ♠Q as a link card to dummy's ♠K. Declarer then discards a diamond on the ♠J in the dummy. Now it is safe to lead trumps. Declarer loses only two hearts and one diamond.

The second tip to simplify entries is:

Tip #2:   Recognize a high card as a link card by using a higher-ranking card as an entry.

Keep an Entry Where it's Needed

Entries are an important consideration in Declarer's Plan, even when taking *sure tricks*. Declarer needs entries to overcome blocked suits and to avoid stranding winners.

When developing tricks through *promotion* or *length*, declarer must be able to reach the winners once they are established. To take a *finesse* and to repeat the finesse if necessary, the declarer has to be on the right side of the table.

To trump a loser, declarer has to be in the right hand to *ruff* the loser and may need entries back to the other hand to ruff more losers. To discard losers, declarer may need entries to establish the extra winner on which to get rid of a loser.

As part of making a plan, declarer walks through the order of play to take advantage of the available entries.

Consider this example. Suppose declarer needs five tricks from these two suits after the ♣J is led:

Dummy (North)
♥ K Q J 10
♣ K 7

West
♣J

Declarer (South)
♥ 7 3
♣ A 5 4 3

Declarer wants to promote three heart winners and take the two club winners. Declarer must win the first trick in the South hand with the ♣A, keeping the ♣K in dummy as an entry to reach the heart winners once the ♥A is driven out.

Let's look at preserving entries in a full deal. South is the declarer in 6♠ and West leads the ♥J:

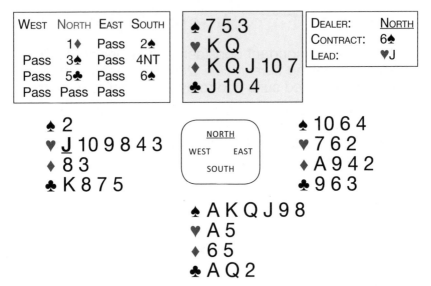

West	North	East	South
	1♦	Pass	2♠
Pass	3♠	Pass	4NT
Pass	5♣	Pass	6♠
Pass	Pass	Pass	

♠ 7 5 3
♥ K Q
♦ K Q J 10 7
♣ J 10 4

Dealer:	North
Contract:	6♠
Lead:	♥J

♠ 2
♥ J 10 9 8 4 3
♦ 8 3
♣ K 8 7 5

♠ 10 6 4
♥ 7 6 2
♦ A 9 4 2
♣ 9 6 3

♠ A K Q J 9 8
♥ A 5
♦ 6 5
♣ A Q 2

Declarer has a diamond and a club loser. Although declarer could try the 50% club finesse to avoid the club loser, a better plan is to discard two clubs on dummy's extra diamond winners.

There will be no problem if the defenders win the first diamond trick since declarer will still have a link card to reach dummy's established diamond winners. What if East *holds up* winning the ♦A until the second round of the suit? Now dummy's remaining diamond winners will be stranded unless declarer has an entry in an outside suit, and the only possibility is the heart suit.

Declarer has to be careful to win the first trick by overtaking dummy's ♥K (or ♥Q) with the ♥A. That leaves the ♥5 as a link card and preserves the ♥Q as an entry to dummy. Declarer draws trumps and then drives out the ♦A. If the defenders don't take the ♦A right away, the ♥K is an entry to the established diamond winners.

The third tip to simplify entries is:

Tip #3: Keep an entry with the suit being developed.

High Card from the Short Side

When taking sure tricks or promoting winners in a suit evenly divided between the two hands, the order the high cards are played doesn't matter. When a suit is divided unevenly between the hands, the order the high cards are played can be important to avoid blocking the suit or stranding winners. Consider the following club layouts:

1)   DUMMY   2)   DUMMY
        ♣ K 5 2   ♣ K 2

       DECLARER   DECLARER
        ♣ A Q 3   ♣ A Q 3

In the first layout, the clubs are divided evenly. Declarer has three winners no matter the order in which the cards are played.

In the second layout, declarer has three tricks. If the first trick is won with the ♣A or ♣Q, however, the suit is blocked. A second trick can be won with the ♣K, but now there is no link card to the winner in declarer's hand. To get three tricks without needing an entry in another suit, the first trick must be won with the ♣K, the high card from the short side, so the ♣2 is preserved as a link card.

The same consideration arises when promoting winners:

3)   DUMMY   4)   DUMMY
        ♣ Q J 4 2   ♣ Q J 10 2

       DECLARER   DECLARER
        ♣ K 10 7 3   ♣ K 3

In the third layout, three tricks can be promoted. You can start by playing a high card from either hand.

In the fourth layout, declarer will need one outside entry to reach the promoted winners assuming the defenders don't win the ♣A right away. If declarer starts with one of dummy's high cards, two outside entries may be needed since the suit can become blocked. Instead, start by playing the ♣K, the high card from the short side.

Consider this deal. South is the declarer in 3NT and West leads the ♦2:

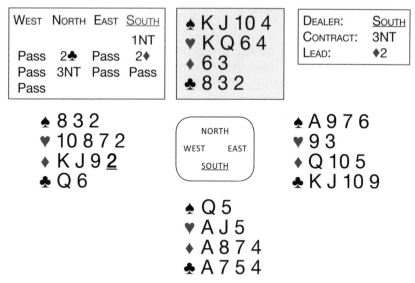

WEST	NORTH	EAST	SOUTH
			1NT
Pass	2♣	Pass	2♦
Pass	3NT	Pass	Pass
Pass			

♠ K J 10 4
♥ K Q 6 4
♦ 6 3
♣ 8 3 2

DEALER:	SOUTH
CONTRACT:	3NT
LEAD:	♦2

♠ 8 3 2
♥ 10 8 7 2
♦ K J 9 2
♣ Q 6

NORTH
WEST   EAST
SOUTH

♠ A 9 7 6
♥ 9 3
♦ Q 10 5
♣ K J 10 9

♠ Q 5
♥ A J 5
♦ A 8 7 4
♣ A 7 5 4

Declarer has six winners: four hearts, a diamond, and a club. Three more tricks are needed, and they can be promoted by driving out the ♠A, but declarer must play the spades in the right order.

The ♦2 lead indicates that West has only a four-card suit, so declarer can win the first trick with the ♦A to avoid a shift to clubs by the defenders. Declarer then plays the ♠Q to start promoting the needed spade winners. If the defenders don't win the ♠A right away, declarer continues with another spade. After the defenders win the ♠A and take three diamond winners, suppose they then lead a club. Declarer wins the ♣A and plays hearts starting with the ♥A and ♥J, keeping the ♥5 as the link card to dummy's two heart winners and the promoted spade winners.

The fourth tip to simplify entries is:

Tip #4:   Play the high card from the short side first when taking sure tricks and promoting tricks.

Take Losses Early

When there aren't enough tricks to make the contract, declarer has to establish the extra winners needed or eliminate the extra losers.

To develop extra winners, declarer may have to give up tricks to the opponents. This will always be the case if declarer is promoting winners and will often happen when developing tricks through length.

Unless the defenders have enough quick tricks to defeat the contract as soon as they gain the lead, it is usually a good idea to lose any necessary tricks early in the play while declarer still has ways to regain the lead in other suits.

Losing tricks early can be necessary when the declarer is trying to preserve the entries needed in order to establish and reach winners in a long suit.

Consider this diamond layout in a notrump contract when there is no outside entry to the dummy:

DUMMY
♦ A K Q 5 2

DECLARER
♦ 6 3

If declarer needs five tricks from this suit, there is no option but to play the ♦A-K-Q and hope the six outstanding diamonds are divided exactly 3-3. That's against the odds, about 36%.

If declarer needs only four tricks from the diamond suit and can afford to give up a trick, then declarer starts the suit by playing a low diamond from both hands, taking the loss early. Declarer is then left with a link card to play to dummy's ♦A-K-Q-5. Dummy's last diamond will be a winner if the missing diamonds are divided either 3-3 or 4-2. The odds of that happening are 84%.

Consider this deal in a suit contract. South is the declarer in 2♠ and West leads the ♦K:

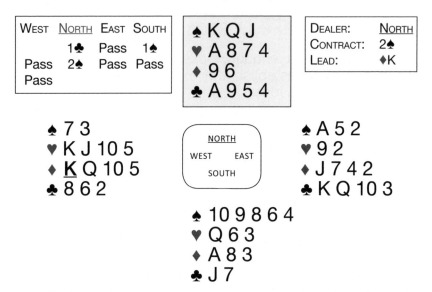

WEST	NORTH	EAST	SOUTH
	1♣	Pass	1♠
Pass	2♠	Pass	Pass
Pass			

♠ K Q J
♥ A 8 7 4
♦ 9 6
♣ A 9 5 4

DEALER:	NORTH
CONTRACT:	2♠
LEAD:	♦K

♠ 7 3
♥ K J 10 5
♦ K Q 10 5
♣ 8 6 2

NORTH
WEST   EAST
SOUTH

♠ A 5 2
♥ 9 2
♦ J 7 4 2
♣ K Q 10 3

♠ 10 9 8 6 4
♥ Q 6 3
♦ A 8 3
♣ J 7

Declarer has six losers: one spade, two hearts, two diamonds and one club. That's one more loser than declarer can afford.

One possibility is to take a heart finesse by leading a low heart toward the ♥Q, hoping East holds the ♥K. That's only a 50% chance. A better plan is to ruff the second diamond loser in dummy. To accomplish this, declarer has to give up a diamond trick to the opponents early.

Suppose declarer wins the first trick with the ♦A and then gives up a diamond. The defenders can win the second round of diamonds and switch to a spade. East wins the ♠A and plays another spade, which declarer wins in the dummy.

The problem is declarer wants to be back in the South hand to play a diamond and has to give up another trick to get there. Then the defenders can lead a third round of spades, removing dummy's last spade. Now there are no spades left in the dummy to trump declarer's last diamond.

Instead, when the ♦K is led, declarer should play a low diamond from both hands, taking the losses early. The defenders can still switch to spades and East can win the ♠A and play another round of spades. Again, declarer wins the second spade in the dummy.

Now, however, declarer plays a low diamond from dummy to get back to the South hand with the ♦A. There is still a spade left in the dummy to rough the third diamond. Declarer makes the contract losing one spade, two hearts, one diamond and one club.

The fifth tip to simplify entries is:

Tip #5:   Take losses early to preserve entries.

PART II

A COLLECTION OF
INSTRUCTIONAL DEALS

The Bridge Quiz

The Bridge Quiz for each deal is on the odd-numbered page. To complete a Bridge Quiz, read:

- Suggested Bidding
- Opening Lead
- Planning the Play

Then consider the question posed in the Bridge Quiz. For the answer, turn the page to read:

- Suggested Play
- Conclusion

For easy reference, put the Declarer's Plan Bookmark, from the front cover, over the even-numbered page that faces the quiz on the odd-numbered page.

After deciding how to play each deal, turn the page over for the answer to the Bridge Quiz. Now put the Five Tips to Simplify Entries Bookmark, from the back cover, over the odd-numbered page that faces the answer as a reminder of the tip being applied.

In the Collection of Instructional Deals, declarer is always South, the opening lead is made by West, and North is the dummy. Usually, the dealer is South.

DEAL #1

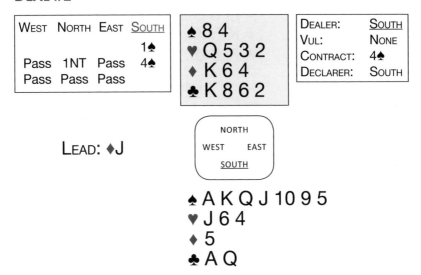

WEST	NORTH	EAST	SOUTH
			1♠
Pass	1NT	Pass	4♠
Pass	Pass	Pass	

♠ 8 4
♥ Q 5 3 2
♦ K 6 4
♣ K 8 6 2

DEALER:	SOUTH
VUL:	NONE
CONTRACT:	4♠
DECLARER:	SOUTH

LEAD: ♦J

NORTH
WEST EAST
SOUTH

♠ A K Q J 10 9 5
♥ J 6 4
♦ 5
♣ A Q

SUGGESTED BIDDING

South has 17 high-card points plus 3 length points for the seven-card spade suit. That's not quite enough to open a strong 2♣, so South starts with 1♠. North, with 8 points and only two spades, responds 1NT. South has a maximum-strength opening bid and takes the partnership right to 4♠.

OPENING LEAD

West leads the ♦J against 4♠.

PLANNING THE PLAY

Declarer can afford three losers. There are three potential heart losers and a diamond loser—one too many. Counting winners, however, there are ten sure tricks: seven spades and three clubs.

BRIDGE QUIZ:

In what order should declarer plan to play the cards to take the ten sure tricks?

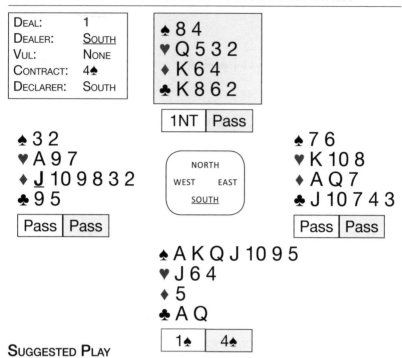

DEAL:	1
DEALER:	SOUTH
VUL:	NONE
CONTRACT:	4♠
DECLARER:	SOUTH

♠ 8 4
♥ Q 5 3 2
♦ K 6 4
♣ K 8 6 2

| 1NT | Pass |

♠ 3 2
♥ A 9 7
♦ J 10 9 8 3 2
♣ 9 5

NORTH
WEST   EAST
SOUTH

♠ 7 6
♥ K 10 8
♦ A Q 7
♣ J 10 7 4 3

| Pass | Pass |

| Pass | Pass |

♠ A K Q J 10 9 5
♥ J 6 4
♦ 5
♣ A Q

| 1♠ | 4♠ |

SUGGESTED PLAY

Declarer needs an entry to dummy to reach the ♣K. The only entry outside the club suit is the ♠8, and the ♠5 is the link card. Declarer has to ruff the second round of diamonds with any spade except the ♠5. Declarer must also draw two rounds of trumps so that the ♣K is not ruffed. Timing is important.

After ruffing the second diamond with a high spade, declarer plays another high spade to draw one round of trumps. Declarer *unblocks* the clubs by playing the ♣A and ♣Q. Now declarer plays the carefully-preserved ♠5 to dummy's ♠8. On this deal, that draws all the outstanding trumps. Declarer takes dummy's ♣K and discards one of the heart losers. Declarer loses only one diamond and two hearts.

CONCLUSION

If you have enough tricks, take them. Be aware of the need for entries and when to draw trumps. Recognize dummy's ♠8 as an entry. Keep the lower-ranking ♠5 as a link card to get to it.

Deal #2

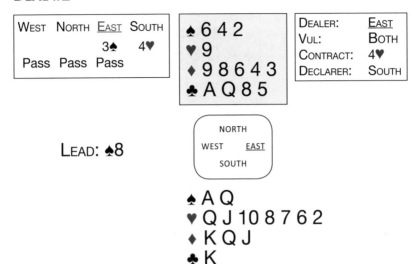

West	North	East	South
		3♠	4♥
Pass	Pass	Pass	

♠ 6 4 2
♥ 9
♦ 9 8 6 4 3
♣ A Q 8 5

Dealer:	East
Vul:	Both
Contract:	4♥
Declarer:	South

Lead: ♠8

NORTH
WEST   EAST
SOUTH

♠ A Q
♥ Q J 10 8 7 6 2
♦ K Q J
♣ K

Suggested Bidding

East opens with a preemptive 3♠ bid. South, with 18 high-card points plus 3 length points for the seven-card heart suit, has more than enough to overcall 4♥, and that ends the auction.

Opening Lead

West leads the ♠8 against 4♥.

Planning the Play

Declarer can afford three losers. After the opening spade lead, it looks as though declarer has only two heart losers and one diamond loser.

Bridge Quiz:

Is there any danger?

If there is, what can be done about it?

DEAL:	2
DEALER:	EAST
VUL:	BOTH
CONTRACT:	4♥
DECLARER:	SOUTH

♠ 6 4 2
♥ 9
♦ 9 8 6 4 3
♣ A Q 8 5

Pass

♠ 8
♥ K 4 3
♦ A 10 7
♣ J 9 7 4 3 2

NORTH
WEST EAST
SOUTH

♠ K J 10 9 7 5 3
♥ A 5
♦ 5 2
♣ 10 6

Pass

3♠ Pass

♠ A Q
♥ Q J 10 8 7 6 2
♦ K Q J
♣ K

4♥

SUGGESTED PLAY

It looks as though declarer has no spade losers after West leads a spade, however, East almost certainly has a seven-card spade suit for the vulnerable 3♠ preempt. That means West's ♠8 is a singleton. If East has an entry, such as the ♥A or ♥K, East can give West a spade ruff.

To guard against this, declarer needs to discard the second spade, to also be out of spades, before starting to draw trumps and giving up the lead. Dummy has extra club winners, but the only entry to dummy is the ♣A. After winning East's ♠K with the ♠A, declarer leads the ♣K and overtakes with the ♣A. Then declarer plays the ♣Q and discards the ♠Q. After that, declarer can start leading trumps.

CONCLUSION

Recognize East as the dangerous opponent and don't draw trumps right away, which would give East the lead. Instead, first discard the ♠Q on dummy's extra club winner, the ♣Q. Recognize the ♣K as a link card to the higher-ranking ♣A in the dummy.

Deal #3

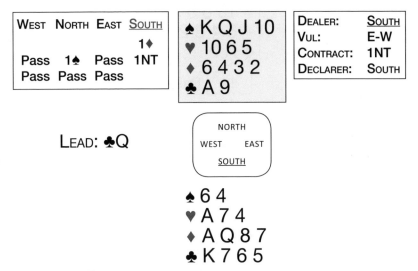

West	North	East	South
			1♦
Pass	1♠	Pass	1NT
Pass	Pass	Pass	

♠ K Q J 10
♥ 10 6 5
♦ 6 4 3 2
♣ A 9

Dealer:	South
Vul:	E-W
Contract:	1NT
Declarer:	South

Lead: ♣Q

NORTH
WEST   EAST
SOUTH

♠ 6 4
♥ A 7 4
♦ A Q 8 7
♣ K 7 6 5

Suggested Bidding

South has 13 high-card points and a balanced hand. That's too weak to open 1NT so South opens a minor suit. The popular agreement is to open 1♦ with four cards in both minors. North responds 1♠. South rebids 1NT to show a minimum-strength, balanced hand. With only 10 high-card points, North settles for partscore.

Opening Lead

West leads the ♣Q against 1NT.

Planning the Play

Declarer needs seven winners. There is one heart trick, one diamond, and two clubs. Three more tricks are needed. The spade suit offers the possibility of promoting three tricks.

Bridge Quiz:

What should declarer play to the first trick and why?

DEAL:	3
DEALER:	SOUTH
VUL:	E-W
CONTRACT:	1NT
DECLARER:	SOUTH

♠ K Q J 10
♥ 10 6 5
♦ 6 4 3 2
♣ A 9

1♠	Pass

NORTH
WEST EAST
SOUTH

♠ A 8
♥ 8 3 2
♦ K 9 5
♣ Q J 10 8 3

Pass	Pass

♠ 9 7 5 3 2
♥ K Q J 9
♦ J 10
♣ 4 2

Pass	Pass

♠ 6 4
♥ A 7 4
♦ A Q 8 7
♣ K 7 6 5

1♦	1NT

SUGGESTED PLAY

If declarer wins the first trick with the ♣A, the contract can be defeated. Suppose declarer then leads spades to promote three extra tricks. West can hold up winning the ♠A and now the two promoted spade winners in dummy are stranded.

Instead, declarer wins the first trick with the ♣K. Declarer then leads spades and, whether or not West holds up winning the ♠A, declarer has an entry to dummy with the ♣A to reach the promoted spade winners.

CONCLUSION

The three extra winners needed can be promoted in the spade suit. Keep an entry, the ♣A, with spades, the suit being promoted.

DEAL #4

West	North	East	South
	1♠	Pass	1NT
Pass	2NT	Pass	3NT
Pass	Pass	Pass	

♠ A K 5 4 3
♥ A 7 5
♦ 10 5
♣ A K 2

DEALER:	NORTH
VUL:	NONE
CONTRACT:	3NT
DECLARER:	SOUTH

LEAD: ♥Q

```
        NORTH
  WEST        EAST
        SOUTH
```

♠ 7 6
♥ K 6
♦ K Q J 3
♣ 9 7 6 4 3

SUGGESTED BIDDING

North has 18 high-card points plus 1 length point for the five-card spade suit, and opens 1♠. South has 9 high-card points plus 1 length point for the five-card club suit and responds 1NT. North raises to 2NT, showing 18-19 points, and a balanced hand. South has enough to accept the invitation and bids 3NT.

OPENING LEAD

West leads the ♥Q against 3NT.

PLANNING THE PLAY

Declarer needs nine tricks. There are two spade tricks, two hearts, and two clubs. Three more tricks are needed.

The spade suit might provide two extra tricks through length if the missing spades are divided 3-3. The diamonds can provide three tricks through promotion. The clubs might provide two extra tricks through length if the missing clubs are divided 3-2.

BRIDGE QUIZ:

Which suit should declarer choose?

What are the challenges?

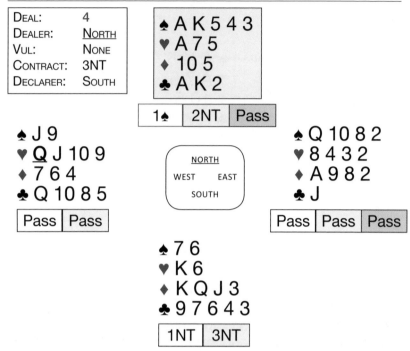

DEAL:	4
DEALER:	NORTH
VUL:	NONE
CONTRACT:	3NT
DECLARER:	SOUTH

♠ A K 5 4 3
♥ A 7 5
♦ 10 5
♣ A K 2

| 1♠ | 2NT | Pass |

♠ J 9
♥ Q J 10 9
♦ 7 6 4
♣ Q 10 8 5

NORTH
WEST   EAST
SOUTH

♠ Q 10 8 2
♥ 8 4 3 2
♦ A 9 8 2
♣ J

| Pass | Pass |

| Pass | Pass | Pass |

♠ 7 6
♥ K 6
♦ K Q J 3
♣ 9 7 6 4 3

| 1NT | 3NT |

SUGGESTED PLAY

Spades or clubs might provide extra tricks. The diamond suit, however, provides a sure way to develop the three extra tricks without establishing any additional tricks for the opponents.

Declarer wins the first trick with dummy's ♥A, keeping the ♥K as an entry to the diamonds. Declarer then leads the ♦10, high card from the short side. If the opponents refuse to take the ♦A right away, declarer continues leading diamonds until the ♦A is driven out. Declarer has two spades, two hearts, two clubs, and three promoted diamond winners.

CONCLUSION

Three extra diamond tricks can be established through promotion. Declarer must win the first trick with the ♥A, keeping the ♥K with the diamonds. When promoting winners in diamonds, declarer starts with the ♦10, high card from the short side first, to avoid blocking the suit.

DEAL #5

WEST	NORTH	EAST	SOUTH
	1♦	Pass	1NT
Pass	Pass	Pass	

♠ 10 8 7
♥ A K
♦ A 8 7 6 3
♣ Q 7 4

DEALER:	NORTH
VUL:	BOTH
CONTRACT:	1NT
DECLARER:	SOUTH

LEAD: ♥J

NORTH
WEST   EAST
SOUTH

♠ K 6 3
♥ Q 4 2
♦ 9 5 2
♣ A 9 5 3

SUGGESTED BIDDING

North opens 1♦ with 13 high-card points plus 1 length point for the five-card diamond suit. South has 9 points but no four-card major. South responds 1NT, showing about 6-9 or 10 points. North passes with a balanced minimum-strength hand.

OPENING LEAD

West leads the ♥J against 1NT.

PLANNING THE PLAY

Declarer needs seven tricks. Declarer has five sure tricks: three hearts, a diamond, and a club. Two more are needed. One possibility is to lead toward the ♣Q, hoping West holds the ♣K and the missing clubs divide 3-3. A much better plan is to try to develop two extra tricks through length in diamonds. It's a 67.8% probability that the opponents diamonds are divided 3-2.

BRIDGE QUIZ:

What are the potential problems?

23

DEAL:	5
DEALER:	NORTH
VUL:	BOTH
CONTRACT:	1NT
DECLARER:	SOUTH

♠ 10 8 7
♥ A K
♦ A 8 7 6 3
♣ Q 7 4

1♦	Pass

NORTH

WEST · EAST

SOUTH

♠ A 9 4
♥ J 10 8 5 3
♦ K Q 10
♣ 10 6

Pass

♠ Q J 5 2
♥ 9 7 6
♦ J 4
♣ K J 8 2

Pass	Pass

♠ K 6 3
♥ Q 4 2
♦ 9 5 2
♣ A 9 5 3

SUGGESTED PLAY

1NT

Declarer has to give up two diamond tricks to get extra tricks through length. Declarer will then need an entry in the dummy to reach the established diamond winners. Since the defenders have led hearts, dummy's heart entries will be gone by the time the diamond suit is established. The only sure remaining entry to dummy is within the diamond suit itself, the ♦A.

After winning the first heart, declarer plays a low diamond from dummy, immediately giving up one of the diamond tricks that must be lost and keeping the ♦A in dummy. If the defenders lead another heart, declarer wins the trick and plays another low diamond from dummy, giving up a second diamond trick. Whatever the defenders do next, declarer gets the lead and plays a diamond to dummy's ♦A and takes the two established diamond winners.

CONCLUSION

Develop two extra diamond tricks using length. Take the losses in diamonds early to preserve the ♦A as an entry to the winners once they are established. Then declarer still has a diamond link card.

DEAL #6

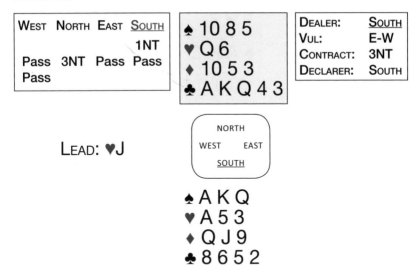

WEST	NORTH	EAST	SOUTH
			1NT
Pass	3NT	Pass	Pass
Pass			

♠ 10 8 5
♥ Q 6
♦ 10 5 3
♣ A K Q 4 3

DEALER:	SOUTH
VUL:	E-W
CONTRACT:	3NT
DECLARER:	SOUTH

LEAD: ♥J

```
        NORTH
WEST            EAST
        SOUTH
```

♠ A K Q
♥ A 5 3
♦ Q J 9
♣ 8 6 5 2

SUGGESTED BIDDING

South has 16 high-card points and a balanced hand, ideal for a 1NT opening bid. North has a balanced hand and 11 high-card points plus 1 length point for the five-card club suit. That's enough to raise to 3NT.

OPENING LEAD

West leads the ♥J against 3NT.

PLANNING THE PLAY

Declarer needs nine tricks. There are three spade winners, a heart winner, and three club winners. The most straightforward plan to get two more winners is to hope the four missing clubs in the defenders' hands are divided either 2-2 or 3-1. That's over a 90% chance and will provide both extra tricks through length.

After winning a trick with the ♥A, declarer will have to rely on the club suit because declarer can't afford to give up the lead.

BRIDGE QUIZ:

What is the potential problem of taking nine tricks?

DEAL:	6
DEALER:	SOUTH
VUL:	E-W
CONTRACT:	3NT
DECLARER:	SOUTH

♠ 10 8 5
♥ Q 6
♦ 10 5 3
♣ A K Q 4 3

3NT

♠ 9 7 6
♥ J 10 8 7 4
♦ A 6 4 2
♣ 9

NORTH

WEST   EAST

SOUTH

♠ J 4 3 2
♥ K 9 2
♦ K 8 7
♣ J 10 7

Pass | Pass

Pass

♠ A K Q
♥ A 5 3
♦ Q J 9
♣ 8 6 5 2

1NT | Pass

SUGGESTED PLAY

Declarer needs to be careful taking the club winners. If declarer plays the ♣A-K-Q and follows with the ♣2, ♣5, and ♣6 from the South hand, declarer will have to win the fourth round of clubs with the ♣8. Now declarer has the lead and has no link card to get to dummy's club winner.

Declarer has to unblock the club suit by playing the ♣8-6-5 under dummy's ♣A-K-Q, preserving the ♣2 to be played when the ♣3 or ♣4 is played from dummy. The ♣3 or ♣4 will then win the fourth trick and declarer will be in the right place, in the dummy, to take the last club trick.

CONCLUSION

Take the sure tricks, being aware of the need for entries to the dummy in clubs. Recognize a low card, the ♣4, as an entry by keeping a lower-ranking card, the ♣2, as the link card. Unblock the ♣8-6-5 under the ♣A-K-Q.

DEAL #7

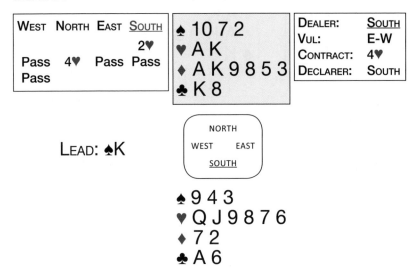

WEST	NORTH	EAST	SOUTH
			2♥
Pass	4♥	Pass	Pass
Pass			

♠ 10 7 2
♥ A K
♦ A K 9 8 5 3
♣ K 8

DEALER:	SOUTH
VUL:	E-W
CONTRACT:	4♥
DECLARER:	SOUTH

LEAD: ♠K

NORTH
WEST   EAST
SOUTH

♠ 9 4 3
♥ Q J 9 8 7 6
♦ 7 2
♣ A 6

SUGGESTED BIDDING

South has only 7 high-card points plus 2 length points for the six-card heart suit. That's not enough to open at the one level but, with a good six-card suit, South can start with a weak 2♥ bid. North has more than enough to raise to game.

OPENING LEAD

West leads the ♠K against 4♥.

PLANNING THE PLAY

Declarer can afford to lose three tricks and, after the opening lead, loses the first three spade tricks. Declarer can afford no more losers.

BRIDGE QUIZ:

In what order should declarer plan to play the cards to take the rest of the tricks?

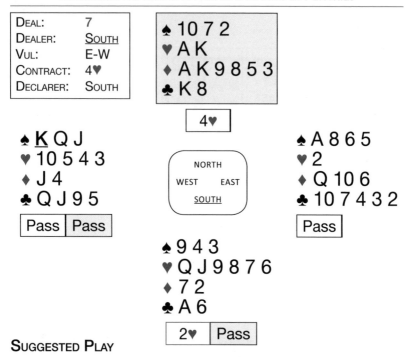

DEAL:	7
DEALER:	SOUTH
VUL:	E-W
CONTRACT:	4♥
DECLARER:	SOUTH

♠ 10 7 2
♥ A K
♦ A K 9 8 5 3
♣ K 8

4♥

♠ K Q J
♥ 10 5 4 3
♦ J 4
♣ Q J 9 5

NORTH
WEST   EAST
SOUTH

♠ A 8 6 5
♥ 2
♦ Q 10 6
♣ 10 7 4 3 2

Pass   Pass

Pass

♠ 9 4 3
♥ Q J 9 8 7 6
♦ 7 2
♣ A 6

2♥   Pass

SUGGESTED PLAY

To take the rest of the tricks, declarer has to draw trumps first. Unfortunately the trump suit is blocked.

The order in which the cards are played is important. After taking the ♥A-K, declarer needs an entry to the South hand to draw any outstanding trumps. It might be dangerous to try to get to the South hand by ruffing the third round of diamonds. A defender may have a singleton diamond, or declarer may get overruffed on the third round of diamonds.

Here's the right order. After West wins the first three spade tricks, and plays the ♣Q, declarer plays the ♣K from dummy. Declarer then draws two rounds of trumps with the ♥A-K. Declarer can use the ♣A as the entry to the South hand to draw the remaining hearts. Declarer takes six hearts, two diamonds, and two clubs to make the contract.

CONCLUSION

Draw trumps, being aware of the need for entries. Keep an entry, the ♣A, with the trump suit, hearts.

DEAL #8

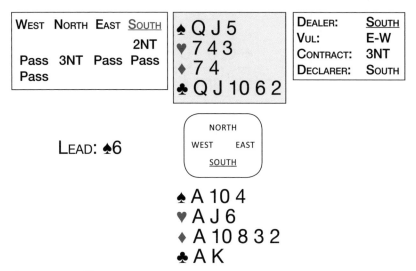

WEST	NORTH	EAST	SOUTH
			2NT
Pass	3NT	Pass	Pass
Pass			

♠ Q J 5
♥ 7 4 3
♦ 7 4
♣ Q J 10 6 2

DEALER:	SOUTH
VUL:	E-W
CONTRACT:	3NT
DECLARER:	SOUTH

LEAD: ♠6

NORTH
WEST   EAST
SOUTH

♠ A 10 4
♥ A J 6
♦ A 10 8 3 2
♣ A K

SUGGESTED BIDDING

South has a balanced hand with 20 high-card points plus 1 length point for the five-card diamond suit. That's ideal for an opening 2NT bid when the partnership range is 20-21 points. North, with 6 high-card points plus 1 length point for the five-card club suit, has enough to raise to game.

OPENING LEAD

West leads the ♠6 against 3NT.

PLANNING THE PLAY

Declarer needs nine tricks. After the spade lead, declarer has two spade winners, a heart, a diamond, and five club tricks. However, the club suit is blocked and there is no immediate entry to reach the club winners in dummy.

BRIDGE QUIZ:

How can the problem be solved?

DEAL:	8
DEALER:	SOUTH
VUL:	E-W
CONTRACT:	3NT
DECLARER:	SOUTH

♠ Q J 5
♥ 7 4 3
♦ 7 4
♣ Q J 10 6 2

3NT

```
        NORTH
   WEST       EAST
        SOUTH
```

♠ K 9 7 6 3
♥ K 8 2
♦ K 6
♣ 8 7 3

Pass | Pass

♠ 8 2
♥ Q 10 9 5
♦ Q J 9 5
♣ 9 5 4

Pass

♠ A 10 4
♥ A J 6
♦ A 10 8 3 2
♣ A K

2NT | Pass

SUGGESTED PLAY

If declarer wins the first trick with one of dummy's spade *honors* or the ♠10 in declarer's hand, declarer will have no entry to dummy's clubs. There will be no link card in spades to get to an entry in dummy. If declarer leads a low spade, West can prevent declarer from reaching dummy by winning the ♠K. The defenders can then hold declarer to at most six tricks: two spades, one heart, one diamond, and two clubs.

Instead, declarer has to win the first trick with the ♠A, keeping the ♠10-4 as link cards. Declarer unblocks clubs by taking the ♣A-K. Then declarer leads a spade. West can win the ♠K, but declarer now has a spade entry to dummy and a link card, the ♠10 or ♣4, to get there. Once in dummy, declarer takes the club winners.

CONCLUSION

If you have enough tricks, take them, being aware of the need for entries. Keep an entry, the ♠Q-J, with the club winners in dummy. Play the ♠A on trick one and keep the lower-ranking link cards, the ♠10 and ♣4 to reach dummy's spade entry.

Deal #9

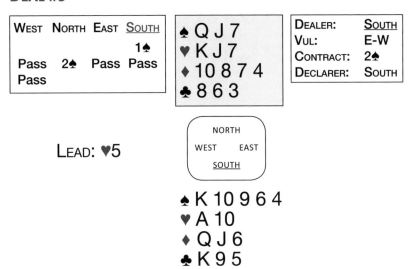

West	North	East	South
			1♠
Pass	2♠	Pass	Pass
Pass			

♠ Q J 7
♥ K J 7
♦ 10 8 7 4
♣ 8 6 3

Dealer:	South
Vul:	E-W
Contract:	2♠
Declarer:	South

Lead: ♥5

```
        NORTH
WEST            EAST
        SOUTH
```

♠ K 10 9 6 4
♥ A 10
♦ Q J 6
♣ K 9 5

Suggested Bidding

South opens 1♠ and North raises to 2♠. South, with a minimum opening bid, passes.

Opening Lead

West leads the ♥5 against 2♠.

Planning the Play

Declarer can afford five losers. There is one spade, two diamonds, and three potential clubs. That's six losers, one too many. Declarer has to get rid of one loser. South could plan to try the club finesse, hoping East holds the ♣A.

Bridge Quiz:

Is there a better choice?

Are there entry problems?

DEAL:	9
DEALER:	SOUTH
VUL:	E-W
CONTRACT:	2♠
DECLARER:	SOUTH

♠ Q J 7
♥ K J 7
♦ 10 8 7 4
♣ 8 6 3

2♠

♠ 8 2
♥ Q 8 6 5 2
♦ K 5 3
♣ A 7 2

NORTH
WEST   EAST
SOUTH

♠ A 5 3
♥ 9 4 3
♦ A 9 2
♣ Q J 10 4

Pass	Pass

Pass

♠ K 10 9 6 4
♥ A 10
♦ Q J 6
♣ K 9 5

1♠	Pass

SUGGESTED PLAY

Instead of relying on the 50% club finesse, declarer has an almost sure thing after the ♥5 lead. The lead gives declarer three heart tricks, and a club loser can be discarded on the extra heart winner in dummy. There will be an entry problem, however, if East plays the ♥9 to the first trick and declarer wins the ♥10. Declarer can take the ♥A, but there is no quick entry to dummy to play the ♥K. If declarer leads a spade or a diamond, East wins and leads the ♣Q, trapping declarer's ♣K and defeating the contract.

Instead, declarer should win the first trick with the ♥A and continue with the ♥10 to dummy's ♥J, finessing against the ♥Q. When the ♥J wins, declarer plays the ♥K and discards a club loser.

CONCLUSION

Develop an extra heart winner with the help of a finesse and use it to discard a club loser. Recognize the ♥J as an entry by keeping a lower-ranking link card, the ♥10. Win the first trick with the ♥A.

DEAL #10

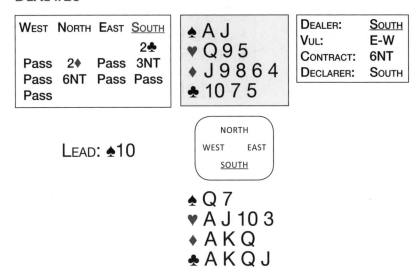

WEST	NORTH	EAST	SOUTH
			2♣
Pass	2♦	Pass	3NT
Pass	6NT	Pass	Pass
Pass			

♠ A J
♥ Q 9 5
♦ J 9 8 6 4
♣ 10 7 5

DEALER:	SOUTH
VUL:	E-W
CONTRACT:	6NT
DECLARER:	SOUTH

LEAD: ♠10

NORTH
WEST   EAST
SOUTH

♠ Q 7
♥ A J 10 3
♦ A K Q
♣ A K Q J

SUGGESTED BIDDING

South, with 26 high-card points, opens a strong, artificial 2♣. North, with 8 high-card points plus 1 length point for the five-card diamond suit, responds 2♦, a waiting bid. South, with a balanced hand, makes a jump rebid to 3NT, showing about 25-27 points. North has enough to take the partnership to 6NT.

OPENING LEAD

West leads the ♠10 against 6NT.

PLANNING THE PLAY

If West holds the ♠K or East holds the ♥K, declarer should have twelve tricks. Unfortunately, on the actual deal, dummy's ♠J loses to East's ♠K, and East returns a spade to dummy's ♠A. Now declarer has to play the heart suit for no losers.

BRIDGE QUIZ:

What is the entry problem in the heart suit?

DEAL:	10
DEALER:	SOUTH
VUL:	E-W
CONTRACT:	6NT
DECLARER:	SOUTH

North
♠ A J
♥ Q 9 5
♦ J 9 8 6 4
♣ 10 7 5

2♦	6NT

West
♠ 10 9 8 6 4
♥ 4 2
♦ 7 5 3
♣ 6 4 3

NORTH

WEST   EAST

SOUTH

East
♠ K 5 3 2
♥ K 8 7 6
♦ 10 2
♣ 9 8 2

Pass	Pass	Pass

Pass	Pass

South
♠ Q 7
♥ A J 10 3
♦ A K Q
♣ A K Q J

2♣	3NT	Pass

SUGGESTED PLAY

Declarer needs four heart tricks and must hope East holds the ♥K. Declarer also needs to repeat the heart finesse three times. If declarer starts with the ♥Q and it wins, declarer is now in the dummy. When declarer takes the second finesse, however, that will be won in the South hand with the ♥J or ♥10. With no further entries to dummy, declarer can't repeat the finesse a third time.

Instead, declarer starts by leading the ♥9 from dummy. The first finesse not only wins, but keeps declarer in the dummy. Declarer continues with the ♥Q. When the second finesse wins, declarer is still in dummy to repeat the finesse a third time.

CONCLUSION

When entries are limited, declarer needs to keep entries on the right side to repeat the finesse. With this heart card combination, declarer has to start by playing the ♥9 and then play the ♥Q to repeat the finesse.

DEAL #11

West	North	East	South
			1NT
Pass	2NT	Pass	3NT
Pass	Pass	Pass	

♠ 9 7 5
♥ 10 7
♦ A Q 4 2
♣ Q J 8 5

Dealer:	South
Vul:	E-W
Contract:	3NT
Declarer:	South

LEAD: ♥5

NORTH
WEST   EAST
SOUTH

♠ A Q J 10
♥ K J
♦ K 9 7 3
♣ K 10 4

SUGGESTED BIDDING

South opens 1NT with a balanced hand and 17 high-card points. North makes an invitational raise to 2NT with 9 high-card points and no four-card or longer major suit. South accepts the invitation with a maximum for the 1NT opening and bids 3NT.

OPENING LEAD

West leads the ♥5 against 3NT.

PLANNING THE PLAY

Declarer needs nine tricks and has one spade, one heart, and three diamonds for a total of five tricks. Diamonds can provide a sixth trick if the five missing diamonds are divided 3-2, as expected. Declarer needs three more tricks. Clubs could provide the three additional tricks through promotion. Declarer could also get three extra tricks from the spade suit with the help of the finesse, hoping East holds the ♠K.

BRIDGE QUIZ:

Should declarer choose clubs or spades to develop the extra tricks needed?

DEAL:	11
DEALER:	SOUTH
VUL:	E-W
CONTRACT:	3NT
DECLARER:	SOUTH

♠ 9 7 5
♥ 10 7
♦ A Q 4 2
♣ Q J 8 5

2NT	Pass

♠ 6 2
♥ A 9 8 5 4
♦ J 6 5
♣ 7 6 3

NORTH

WEST   EAST

SOUTH

♠ K 8 4 3
♥ Q 6 3 2
♦ 10 8
♣ A 9 2

Pass	Pass

Pass	Pass

♠ A Q J 10
♥ K J
♦ K 9 7 3
♣ K 10 4

1NT	3NT

SUGGESTED PLAY

Declarer can't afford to promote clubs since it gives up the lead to the ♣A and the defenders will take their heart tricks. So, declarer needs to rely on the repeated spade finesse and be careful with entries. If East holds four or more spades, declarer must take three finesses against the ♠K. Three entries are needed. The ♦A and ♦Q are two sure entries. Where's the third? Dummy's ♦4 is the third entry, provided declarer keeps the ♦3 as a link card.

Declarer wins the ♥K, takes the ♦K, playing the ♦2 from dummy. Declarer then plays the ♦9 (or ♦7) to dummy's ♦Q and takes the first spade finesse. When this works, declarer leads the ♦7 to dummy's ♦A and takes a second finesse. Finally, the carefully preserved ♦3 is led to dummy's ♦4 and declarer takes a third spade finesse.

CONCLUSION

The plan is to develop three extra spade tricks using the repeated spade finesse. Recognize a low card as an entry, dummy's ♦4, by keeping a lower-ranking link card, the ♦3 in declarer's hand.

DEAL #12

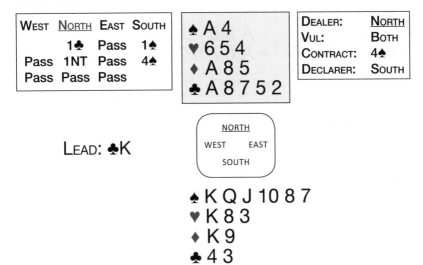

WEST	NORTH	EAST	SOUTH
	1♣	Pass	1♠
Pass	1NT	Pass	4♠
Pass	Pass	Pass	

♠ A 4
♥ 6 5 4
♦ A 8 5
♣ A 8 7 5 2

DEALER:	NORTH
VUL:	BOTH
CONTRACT:	4♠
DECLARER:	SOUTH

LEAD: ♣K

```
        NORTH
  WEST       EAST
        SOUTH
```

♠ K Q J 10 8 7
♥ K 8 3
♦ K 9
♣ 4 3

SUGGESTED BIDDING

North opens 1♣ and South responds 1♠. North rebids 1NT to show a minimum balanced hand with about 12-14 points. South, with 12 high-card points plus 2 length points for the six-card spade suit, has enough to take the partnership to game. South expects there is at least an eight-card spade fit since North has shown a balanced hand.

OPENING LEAD

West leads the ♣K against 4♠.

PLANNING THE PLAY

Declarer can only afford three losers. There are three potential heart losers and a club loser, one too many. One possibility is to plan to lead toward the ♥K, hoping East holds the ♥A, a 50% chance.

BRIDGE QUIZ:

What card should declarer play from the dummy after the ♣K is led?

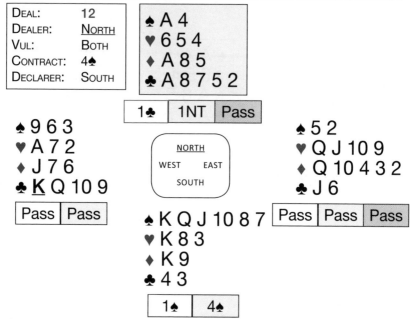

DEAL:	12
DEALER:	NORTH
VUL:	BOTH
CONTRACT:	4♠
DECLARER:	SOUTH

♠ A 4
♥ 6 5 4
♦ A 8 5
♣ A 8 7 5 2

1♣	1NT	Pass

♠ 9 6 3
♥ A 7 2
♦ J 7 6
♣ K Q 10 9

NORTH
WEST   EAST
SOUTH

♠ 5 2
♥ Q J 10 9
♦ Q 10 4 3 2
♣ J 6

Pass	Pass

♠ K Q J 10 8 7
♥ K 8 3
♦ K 9
♣ 4 3

Pass	Pass	Pass

1♠	4♠

SUGGESTED PLAY

Declarer should play a low club from dummy after the ♣K is led, keeping West, the safe opponent, on lead. If declarer wins the ♣A, planning to later give up a club, there are two problems. East, the dangerous opponent, could gain the lead with the ♣J and play a heart to trap the ♥K before clubs are established. There's a problem.

Instead, declarer lets West win the first trick with the ♣K. If West shifts to a diamond, declarer wins the ♦K, plays a club to dummy's ♣A, and ruffs a club high. When clubs divide 4-2, declarer draws two rounds of spades, ending in dummy with the ♠A, and ruffs another club, establishing dummy's last club as a winner. Declarer draws the last trump, crosses to dummy's ♦A, and discards a heart on the club winner. Declarer can try the heart finesse for an overtrick, although it doesn't work on this deal.

CONCLUSION

Develop clubs through length to discard one or more heart losers. Take a loss early in clubs to keep the safe opponent on lead and to preserve the ♣A as an entry.

DEAL #13

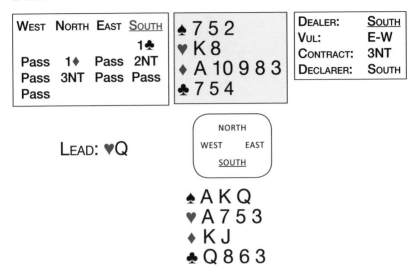

WEST	NORTH	EAST	SOUTH
			1♣
Pass	1♦	Pass	2NT
Pass	3NT	Pass	Pass
Pass			

♠ 7 5 2
♥ K 8
♦ A 10 9 8 3
♣ 7 5 4

DEALER:	SOUTH
VUL:	E-W
CONTRACT:	3NT
DECLARER:	SOUTH

LEAD: ♥Q

NORTH
WEST   EAST
SOUTH

♠ A K Q
♥ A 7 5 3
♦ K J
♣ Q 8 6 3

SUGGESTED BIDDING

South has a balanced hand with 19 high-card points, too strong to open 1NT but not strong enough for 2NT. South opens 1♣. When North responds 1♦, South jumps to 2NT to show a balanced hand with 18-19 points. North, with 7 high-card points plus 1 length point for the five-card diamond suit, has enough to accept the invitation and bids 3NT.

OPENING LEAD

West leads the ♥Q against 3NT.

PLANNING THE PLAY

Declarer needs nine tricks and has three spades, two hearts, and two diamonds. Two more tricks are needed. They aren't coming from spades or hearts and aren't likely coming from clubs. So, the diamond suit will need to provide two additional winners.

BRIDGE QUIZ:

How are you going to play the diamonds?

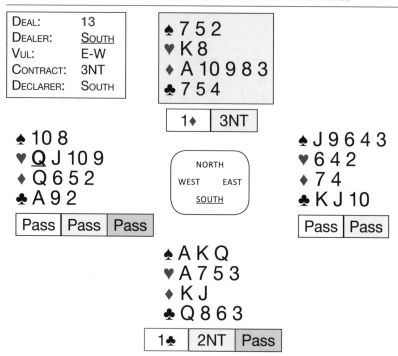

DEAL:	13
DEALER:	SOUTH
VUL:	E-W
CONTRACT:	3NT
DECLARER:	SOUTH

♠ 7 5 2
♥ K 8
♦ A 10 9 8 3
♣ 7 5 4

| 1♦ | 3NT |

♠ 10 8
♥ Q J 10 9
♦ Q 6 5 2
♣ A 9 2

NORTH
WEST   EAST
SOUTH

♠ J 9 6 4 3
♥ 6 4 2
♦ 7 4
♣ K J 10

| Pass | Pass | Pass |

| Pass | Pass |

♠ A K Q
♥ A 7 5 3
♦ K J
♣ Q 8 6 3

| 1♣ | 2NT | Pass |

SUGGESTED PLAY

Missing the ♦Q, declarer could take a finesse by leading the ♦K and following with the ♦J, playing low from dummy if West plays low. Even if the finesse works, as on the actual deal, that only provides one extra diamond trick unless the ♦Q falls on the third round of diamonds.

Declarer guarantees the contract by winning the first trick with the ♥A, taking a trick with the ♦K, leading the ♦J, and overtaking with dummy's ♦A. When the ♦Q doesn't fall, declarer can promote two diamond tricks by driving out the ♦Q. The ♥K is an entry to reach the promoted diamond winners in dummy. That's nine tricks: three spades, two hearts, and four diamonds.

CONCLUSION

Two extra diamond tricks can be developed using promotion. Keep an entry, the ♥K, with the suit being developed, diamonds. Recognize a high card as a link card, the ♦J, by using a higher card, the ♦A, as an entry.

DEAL #14

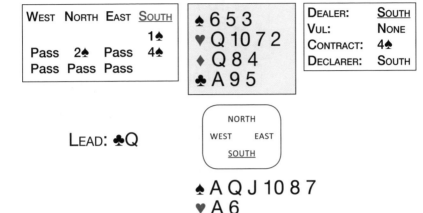

WEST	NORTH	EAST	SOUTH
			1♠
Pass	2♠	Pass	4♠
Pass	Pass	Pass	

♠ 6 5 3
♥ Q 10 7 2
♦ Q 8 4
♣ A 9 5

DEALER:	SOUTH
VUL:	NONE
CONTRACT:	4♠
DECLARER:	SOUTH

LEAD: ♣Q

```
        NORTH
 WEST         EAST
        SOUTH
```

♠ A Q J 10 8 7
♥ A 6
♦ A J
♣ K 8 3

SUGGESTED BIDDING

South has 19 high-card points plus 2 length points for the six-card spade suit. That's not quite enough to open a strong 2♣, so South starts with 1♠. North, with 8 high-card points and three-card support for spades, raises to 2♠. South, with a maximum-strength opening bid, now takes the partnership to 4♠.

OPENING LEAD

West leads the ♣Q against 4♠.

PLANNING THE PLAY

Declarer can afford three losers. There are four potential losers, one in each suit. The spade or the diamond loser might be avoided with the help of a finesse. A heart loser could be discarded if there is an extra diamond winner in dummy. A club loser could also be discarded on an extra diamond winner. If West has the ♥K, an extra heart winner can be established in dummy. With all these possibilities, the only entry to dummy is the ♣A.

BRIDGE QUIZ:

Should the ♣A be used to take a spade finesse, a diamond finesse or to reach a winner in dummy?

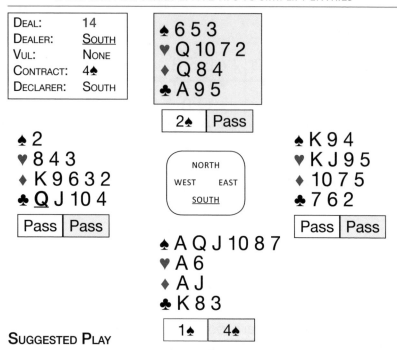

DEAL:	14
DEALER:	SOUTH
VUL:	NONE
CONTRACT:	4♠
DECLARER:	SOUTH

♠ 6 5 3
♥ Q 10 7 2
♦ Q 8 4
♣ A 9 5

| 2♠ | Pass |

♠ 2
♥ 8 4 3
♦ K 9 6 3 2
♣ Q J 10 4

NORTH
WEST   EAST
SOUTH

♠ K 9 4
♥ K J 9 5
♦ 10 7 5
♣ 7 6 2

| Pass | Pass |

| Pass | Pass |

♠ A Q J 10 8 7
♥ A 6
♦ A J
♣ K 8 3

| 1♠ | 4♠ |

SUGGESTED PLAY

Using the entry for a spade finesse works only if East has a singleton or doubleton ♠K. On this deal, even though the ♠K is well-placed, a second entry is needed to repeat the finesse. Using the entry for a diamond finesse works only if East holds the ♦K. If the finesse loses, the defenders can lead another club to establish a club winner. Now declarer can't reach dummy to make use of the ♦Q. Playing hearts works only if West holds the ♥K or ♥J, and declarer can guess which.

A much better use for the ♣A is as an entry once dummy's ♦Q has been promoted into a winner. Declarer wins the ♣K, saving the ♣A, the only entry to dummy. Then declarer plays the ♦A followed by the ♦J. This gives up a trick to the ♦K but promotes dummy's ♦Q into a winner. Declarer uses the ♣A to reach dummy and discard either a club or heart loser on the ♦Q.

CONCLUSION

The plan is to promote a winner in diamonds on which to discard a loser. Keep an entry, the ♣A, with the suit being promoted, diamonds, by winning the first trick with the ♣K.

Deal #15 – Famous Deal

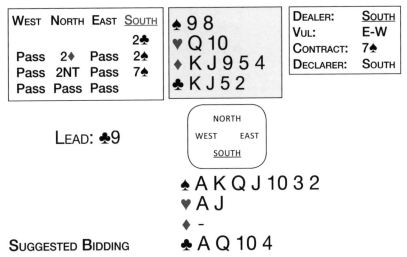

West	North	East	South
			2♣
Pass	2♦	Pass	2♠
Pass	2NT	Pass	7♠
Pass	Pass	Pass	

♠ 9 8
♥ Q 10
♦ K J 9 5 4
♣ K J 5 2

Dealer:	South
Vul:	E-W
Contract:	7♠
Declarer:	South

Lead: ♣9

NORTH
WEST   EAST
SOUTH

♠ A K Q J 10 3 2
♥ A J
♦ -
♣ A Q 10 4

Suggested Bidding

South opens with a strong artificial 2♣ bid with 21 high-card points plus 3 length points for the seven-card spade suit. North responds with a 2♦ waiting bid, and South now shows the spade suit.

North's 2NT bid shows some values since 3♣, the cheaper minor, would be a negative bid. The auction could continue in many ways at this point. Assume South bids a grand slam in spades, hoping North has the ♣K and ♥K. That's the contract that was actually reached when this famous deal was played.

Opening Lead

West leads the ♣9 against 7♠.

Planning the Play

Declarer can't afford any losers. With only one potential heart loser, declarer could simply draw trump and rely on the 50% heart finesse. But there is another chance. If the defenders' diamonds divide 4-4 or the ♦A falls in two or three rounds, a diamond winner can be developed on which to discard the ♥J.

Bridge Quiz:

In what order should declarer play the cards to maximize the chances of making the contract?

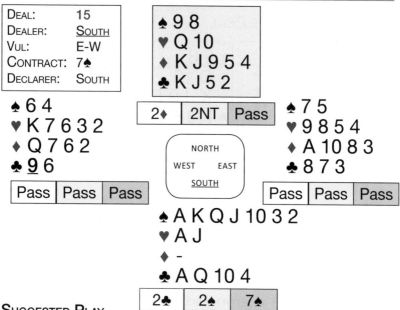

DEAL: 15
DEALER: SOUTH
VUL: E-W
CONTRACT: 7♠
DECLARER: SOUTH

♠ 9 8
♥ Q 10
♦ K J 9 5 4
♣ K J 5 2

♠ 6 4
♥ K 7 6 3 2
♦ Q 7 6 2
♣ 9 6

| 2♦ | 2NT | Pass |

NORTH
WEST   EAST
SOUTH

♠ 7 5
♥ 9 8 5 4
♦ A 10 8 3
♣ 8 7 3

| Pass | Pass | Pass |

| Pass | Pass | Pass |

♠ A K Q J 10 3 2
♥ A J
♦ -
♣ A Q 10 4

| 2♣ | 2♠ | 7♠ |

SUGGESTED PLAY

Declarer wins the first trick with the ♣A. The ♠2 to dummy's ♠8 allows declarer to lead a diamond and ruff high. The ♠3 to dummy's ♠9 draws all the trumps and allows declarer to ruff a second diamond. Declarer leads the ♣Q and overtakes with the ♣K, noting that the defenders' clubs have divided 3-2. Declarer ruffs a third diamond.

Since the ♦A hasn't appeared, declarer plays the ♣10 and overtakes with dummy's ♣J to lead a fourth diamond. This time the ♦A appears. Declarer crosses to dummy once more by playing the ♣4 to dummy's ♣5 and takes the ♦K, discarding the heart loser. If the ♦A didn't fall or clubs divided 4-1, declarer could then fall back on the heart finesse.

CONCLUSION

Declarer can try to establish the ♦K as a winner. Otherwise, the heart finesse can be taken. Keep entries with the diamonds in the dummy. Recognize low cards as entries, the ♠8, ♠9, and ♣5, by keeping lower-ranking link cards, the ♠2, ♠3, and ♣4. Recognize high cards as link cards, the ♣Q and ♣10, by keeping higher-ranking cards as entries, the ♣K and ♣J.

This is a famous deal. Alfred Sheinwold reached 7♠ and played the deal exactly as suggested.

DEAL #16 – FAMOUS DEAL

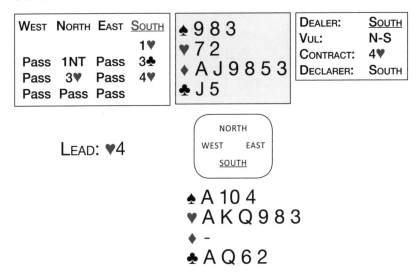

WEST	NORTH	EAST	SOUTH
			1♥
Pass	1NT	Pass	3♣
Pass	3♥	Pass	4♥
Pass	Pass	Pass	

♠ 9 8 3
♥ 7 2
♦ A J 9 8 5 3
♣ J 5

DEALER:	SOUTH
VUL:	N-S
CONTRACT:	4♥
DECLARER:	SOUTH

LEAD: ♥4

NORTH
WEST   EAST
SOUTH

♠ A 10 4
♥ A K Q 9 8 3
♦ -
♣ A Q 6 2

SUGGESTED BIDDING

South has 19 high-card points plus 2 length points for the six-card heart suit. That's not quite enough for a 2♣ opening so South opens 1♥. North responds 1NT with 6 high-card points plus 2 length points for the six-card diamond suit. South has enough for a jump shift to 3♣. North gives preference back to 3♥ and South continues by bidding 4♥.

OPENING LEAD

West leads the ♥4 against 4♥.

PLANNING THE PLAY

Declarer has two spade losers and two club losers. If there was an entry to dummy, declarer could discard a loser on the ♦A.

BRIDGE QUIZ:

Is there any way declarer can create an entry to dummy?

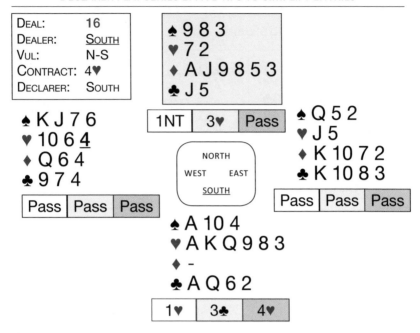

SUGGESTED PLAY

After winning the first heart trick, declarer could try leading a low club to dummy's ♣J, hoping West has the ♣K, and the ♣J is now an entry to the ♦A. Unfortunately, East wins the ♣K and returns another heart. Now there are no hearts left in the dummy and declarer can't trump a club loser or a spade loser.

To get to dummy's ♦A, declarer must win the first heart trick and make the unusual play of leading the ♣Q at trick two. This creates a problem for the defenders. If East takes the ♣K, the ♣J is an entry to dummy and a club loser can be discarded on the ♦A. If East doesn't take the ♣K, declarer can then play to the ♣A and trump the third club in dummy to discard a club loser on the ♦A.

CONCLUSION

Declarer can force the defenders to provide an entry to dummy's ♦A by leading the ♣Q at trick two.

This is a famous deal. Singer Lainie Kazan bid and played the deal exactly as suggested.

Glossary

Blocked—A suit in which the winners cannot be taken immediately because of entry problems. (Page 3)

Entry—A way to get from one hand to the opposite hand. (Page 1)

Finesse—A method of building extra tricks by trapping an opponent's high card(s). (page 5)

Hold Up—Letting the opponents win a trick that you could win. (Page 6)

Honor—An ace, king, queen, jack, or ten. (Page 30)

L'Entry—The combination of a link card and an entry. (Page 1)

Length—The number of cards held in a suit. Also, developing tricks by exhausting the cards that the opponents hold in a suit. (Page 5)

Link Card—A card that can be led to a winner (entry) in the opposite hand. (Page 1)

Loser—A trick that might be lost to the opponents. (Page 4)

Overtake—Play a higher card in the suit led, typically when partner's card was already winning the trick. (Page 3)

Partially Blocked—A suit in which tricks can be taken or established only by sacrificing a potential winner. (Page 3)

Promotion—Developing one or more cards into winners by driving out any higher-ranking cards held by the opponents. (Page 5)

Ruff—Play a trump to a trick when holding no cards in the suit led. Same as trumping. (Page 5)

Stranded—Potential winners in one hand that cannot be reached from the other hand. (Page 1)

Suit Combination—A combined holding in a suit between the partnership hands. (Page 1)

Sure Trick—A trick that can be taken without giving up the lead to the opponents. (Page 5)

Unblock—Play or discard a high card that is preventing taking winners in a suit. (Page 16)

Winner—A card held by one of the players that will win a trick when it is played. (Page 1)

Notes

Notes